T0348817

THE MARCUS AURELIUS BOOK OF QUOTES

THE MARCUS AURELIUS BOOK OF QUOTES

Over 150 Quotes from the
Greatest Stoic of All Time

NICK BENAS, USMC &
KORTNEY YASENKA, LCMHC

 **hatherleigh**

Hatherleigh Press, Ltd.
62545 State Highway 10
Hobart, NY 13788, USA
hatherleighpress.com

》》 hatherleigh

THE MARCUS AURELIUS BOOK OF QUOTES

Library of Congress Cataloging-in-Publication Data is available.

ISBN: 978-1-961293-25-0

Printed in the United States

The authorized representative in the EU for product safety and compliance is Catarina Astrom, Blästorpsvägen 14, 276 35 Borrby, Sweden. info@hatherleighpress.com

10 9 8 7 6 5 4 3 2 1

For Dian, Ed, Shelly, Noah, and Kiyon,
my beautiful beacons in the storms and
calms of life.
—Nick

For my sister, Kristin, and brother
Aaron, the two people who know me
better than anyone else.
—Kortney

Contents

Introduction

CONTAINED WITHIN THESE PAGES are words never meant for public eyes, but here they stand—insights meant solely for one individual.

Marcus Aurelius, the philosopher-king of ancient Rome—last and greatest of the Five Good Emperors.

Marcus had power, riches, and people at his beck and call. Yet for all his fame and might, he was still as human as the rest of us, susceptible to getting stuck, becoming immobilized by fear, and at times, struggling to keep his head above water.

Despite his well-known preference for solitude, his most enduring legacy comes courtesy of his most personal musings: his journal, his greatest treasure. Marcus' private writings reflect his constant battle to navigate his country in a swiftly changing world. The text has been passed down through the centuries, much cherished, oft quoted, frequently translated and lovingly expressed in authentic oratory.

The following text is our gift to you, a carefully curated collection of quotations. We, of course, are only students of stoicism—hobbyists of a sort—and our growth process still ongoing. For this reason, *The Marcus Aurelius Book of Quotes* was crafted to be compact, easily digestible, and a wonderful companion to *The Stoicism Book of Quotes*.

Most people are looking for ways to improve their lives, to be healthier and happier. Many more are constantly searching for answers to questions like, "What will make me feel more fulfilled?" "What will lead to stronger relationships?" "What will contribute to a more successful life and an overall better existence?" "What can help me enjoy a life free of anxiety and depression?"

Aurelius' observations on daily living may be the key to a balanced, more fulfilled, and happier life. The ways in which Marcus Aurelius lived his life are the truest examples of what it truly means to be a Stoic. Viewing situations through this mindset allowed him to gain more control over his own thoughts, feelings, and behaviors; may it now do the same for you.

The wisdom of the philosopher's words and the example he set still resonate today. Our hope is that the ideas of Marcus Aurelius, which time has seen fit to preserve, will help you find meaning and purpose in life.

But the interpretation and use of his insights are ultimately up to you.

Marcus Aurelius & Stoicism

"The art of life is more like the wrestler's art than the dancer's, in respect of this, that it should stand ready and firm to meet onsets which are sudden and unexpected."

—MARCUS AURELIUS

MARCUS AURELIUS WAS BORN Marcus Aurelius Antoninus on the 26th day of April, 121 AD. Growing up in great wealth and nobility in Rome, Italy, his was a life of privilege. His father was Marcus Annius Verus, a prestigious Roman *praetor*—a powerful political figure with great authority in Rome. He passed away when Marcus was just three years of age. His mother, Domitia Lucilla, was a descendant of a great noble family. She was an avid student of Greek language and culture, and many believe she selected tutors for Marcus based on their Stoic pedigree.

After his father's death, Marcus Aurelius was later adopted by his uncle, Antoninus Pius, who has been credited with curating his development into adulthood. He also benefitted greatly from an association with Emperor Hadrian who was responsible for lining him up for succession in Rome. Throughout *Meditations,* a collection of personal writings penned during his imperial reign, Marcus thanks his many tutors for the tutelage, expressing great gratitude.

Throughout his works, we see that even as a young boy he was possessed of sound character and moral integrity. Aurelius was a bright and laborious young lad, a polymath known to embrace the hardened life by choice, just like the Stoics before him. He was educated in military tactics, law, philosophy, rhetoric and stoicism. He was as renowned a soldier as he was an Emperor, surviving many campaigns in various theatres of war. He died at the age of 58, having outlived most of his children, and died in a place named Sirmium, a Roman province in what is now Serbia.

But rather than concern ourselves with his long list of achievements, our focus is on the cultivated mindset of practical Stoicism that empowered Marcus Aurelius to succeed and inspire where so many others would have failed.

Stoicism is an ancient philosophy based on the premise that you can alter your mindset to focus only on what is within your control and consciously choose how to respond based on this knowledge. The Stoic mindset holds in high regard an individual's capacity to be in control of their reactions. Being Stoic is not being void of emotions; rather it is simply not allowing your emotions to control you. Marcus Aurelius knew the powerful effect a Stoic mindset can have on an individual.

To assist you on your journey to living a more Stoic life, we have arranged this book into seven concise chapters, each focusing on a specific aspect of daily living:

Change discusses the ever-shifting experiences and situations that we all encounter throughout our lifetimes. The wise words and thoughts of Marcus Aurelius are referenced here to help you navigate these changes with a Stoic mindset, one which will help you better acknowledge, accept, and cope with the ebb and flow of fate.

Dealing With People draws on writings found in Marcus Aurelius' personal diary to better understand the potential influences that others may have on us. This chapter also discusses the importance of dealing with people in a Stoic way and the benefits that the Stoic mindset has to offer when communicating, interacting, and responding to others.

Chasing Fame is devoted to prioritizing what's most important in life. The Stoic quotes in this chapter encourage us to find purpose and meaning rather than fleeting attention and adoration.

Living With Nature encompasses the natural world as well as the universe as a whole. The Stoic mindset and Marcus Aurelius' way of living strongly emphasizes that the ultimate goal in life is to live in agreement with nature.

Rules For Living Well puts the key Stoic virtues into practice and exemplifies the importance of living a life centered around a Stoic mindset.

This mode of thought is what allows us to focus on only those things within our control, giving us a greater sense of balance and well-being.

Life is Short and **On Death**, the final two chapters, highlight the inevitable fact that nothing lasts forever. Seek to gain a greater appreciation for all life and its offerings by acknowledging this concept. Allow the writings of Marcus Aurelius to motivate you to take action and create a life worth living. Time is precious and the Stoic mindset gives you the ability to cherish each moment as the priceless gift it really is.

I

CHANGE

CHANGE IS AN INEVITABLE and necessary part of life, but often the word carries a negative connotation. An understandable sentiment—change can be difficult at the best of times and overwhelming at the worst. But for all that, change remains an essential part of living. Marcus Aurelius said it best: "Frightened by change? But what can exist without it?"

If you catch yourself thinking of change in a negative way, try altering your mindset. Even if you're unable to change your situation, you can always change how you think and feel about it. Embracing this kind of positive, optimistic mindset instills in us a sense of responsibility for our own actions and choices. Reminding ourselves, especially during difficult times, that we can always choose to adapt to situations by acknowledging and accepting our circumstances and then focusing on what is within our control, such as your attitude and approach, can help you feel better and become more resilient.

That is not to say that change won't impact you, even negatively. But when change is something outside of our control, as it so often is, we must learn how to acknowledge it and welcome it. By doing so, you trade a pointless bid for control for a greater sense of agency, which will lead you to greater acceptance.

View change with Marcus Aurelius in mind. Identify all the positive aspects that come with change, such as new beginnings, new opportunities, and a chance for self-growth. Beautiful things can happen as a result of change. Keep an open-mind and let Stoicism guide you on your new path.

"Let not future things disturb you, for you will come to them, if it shall be necessary, having with you the same reason which now you use for present things."

"All things are implicated with one another, and the bond is holy; and there is hardly anything unconnected with any other thing. For things have been coordinated, and they combine to form the same universe [order]. For there is one universe made up of all things, and one god who pervades all things, and one substance, and one law, [one] common reason in all intelligent animals, and one truth; if indeed there is also one perfection for all animals which are of the same stock and participate in the reason."

"About pain: the pain which is intolerable carries us off; but that which lasts a long time is tolerable; and the mind maintains its own tranquility by retiring into itself, and the ruling faculty is not made worse. But the parts which are harmed by pain, let them, if they can, give their opinion about it."

"All things are changing: and you yourself are in continuous mutation and in a manner in continuous destruction, and the whole universe too."

"Nature which governs the whole will soon change all things you see, and out of their substance will make other things, and again other things from the substance of them, in order that the world may be ever new."

"Look round at the courses of the stars, as if you were going along with them; and constantly consider the changes of the elements into one another; for such thoughts purge away the filth of the terrene life."

"Do you dread change? What can come without it? What can be pleasant or more proper to the universal nature? Can you heat your bath unless wood undergoes a change? Can you be fed unless a change is wrought upon your food? Can any useful thing be done without changes?"

"For those too are triflers who have wearied themselves in life by their activity, and yet have no object to which to direct every movement, and, in a word, all their thoughts."

"Think now of your grandfather, then under your mother, then under your father; and, as you find there many other alterations, changes, and endings, ask yourself: Is there anything to dread here? Thus neither is there anything to dread in the cessation, ending, and change of your whole life?"

"Consider the past; such great changes of political supremacies; you may foresee also the things which will be."

"Everything which happens is as familiar and well known as the rose in spring and the fruit in summer; for such is a disease, and death, and calumny, and treachery, and whatever else delights fools or vexes them."

"Give yourself time to learn something new and good and cease to be whirled around."

"It is no evil for things to undergo change, and no good for things to subsist in consequence of change."

"The parts of the whole, everything, I mean, which is naturally comprehended in the universe, must of necessity perish; but let this be understood in this sense, that they must undergo change. But if this is naturally both an evil and a necessity for the parts, the whole would not continue to exist in good condition, the parts being subject to change and constitute so as to perish in various ways."

"Time is like a river made up of the events which happen, and a violent stream; for as soon as a thing has been seen, it is carried away too."

"For whether did nature herself design to do evil to the things which are parts of herself, and to make them subject to evil and of necessity fall into evil, or have such results happen without her knowing it? Both these suppositions, indeed, are incredible this man should even drop the term nature, and should speak of these things as natural, even then it would be ridiculous to affirm at the same time that the parts of the hole are in their nature subject to change, and at that same time to be surprised or vexed as if something were happening contrary to nature, particularly as the dissolution of things is into those things of which each thing is composed.

For there is either a dispersion of the elements out of which everything has been compounded or a change from the solid to the earthy and from the area to the aerial, so that these parts are taken back into the universal reason, whether this at certain periods is consumed by fire or renewed by eternal changes. and do not imagine that these solid and the airy part belong to you from the time of generation. For all this received it's accretion only yesterday and the day before, as one may say, from the food in the air which is inspired. this, then, which has received, changes, not that which your mother brought forth. But suppose that this implicates the very much with that other part, which is the peculiar quality, this is nothing in fact in the way of objection to what it said."

"The unripe grape, the ripe bunch, the dried grape, are all changes, not into nothing, but into something which exists not yet."

"And all our assent is changeable; for where is the man who never changes?"

"Some things are hurrying into existence, and other things are hurrying out of it; and of that which is coming into existence part is already extinguished. Motions and changes are continually renewing the world, just as the uninterrupted course of times is always renewing the infinite duration of the ages."

"That is for the good of each thing, which the universal nature brings to each. And it is for it's good at the time when nature brings it."

"All things are change, yet we need not fear anything new."

"Consider whence each thing is come, and of what it consists, and into what it changes, and what kind of a thing it will be when it has changed, and that it will sustain no harm."

"Be though erect, or be made erect."

"Eudaemonia is a good daemon, or a good thing. What then art you doing here, O imagination? Go away, I entreat you by the gods, as you didst come, for I want you not. But you art come according to your old fashion. I am not angry with you: only go away."

Challenge: Each day, identify one positive change that occurred during the last 24 hours. This change can be of any magnitude. Concentrate on retraining your brain to view change as a good thing.

II

DEALING WITH PEOPLE

THE ABILITY TO SUCCESSFULLY deal with others comes down to our ability to focus only on what is within your control. Your responses, your reactions, your judgments, your decisions, and your mindset—these are all things within your control. Other people and their behaviors, their thoughts and actions, are *not* within your control. The sooner you come to this realization, the better.

Choose to surround yourself with positive people who enhance your overall well-being. Focus your energy on supportive people who accept you for who you are and who make you feel good about yourself. Don't waste your energy on people who bring you down with negativity and judgment. While you are not in control of others, their opinions or their actions, you can still curate your social interactions to prioritize the people who improve your life. This is what it means to embrace the Stoic mindset, to take full control of what you can affect and accept what you can't. You are in control of yourself, and that is what matters most. Aim to put your responses and reactions in the forefront of your mind. Concern yourself less with others and their issues to better focus on the impact you can have on others.

To be successful and find balance, align yourself with others who share the same virtues as you. This is not always possible, so be mindful of differences and express empathy when needed. Draw from the virtues Marcus Aurelius lived by to help you navigate difficult situations and interactions with others.

"The dispute then, he said, is not about any common matter, but about being mad or not."

"Every moment think steadily as a Roman and a man to do what you have in hand with perfect and simple dignity, and feeling of affection, and freedom, and justice, and to give yourself relief from all other thoughts."

"Enter into every man's ruling faculty; and also let every other man enter into thine."

"A slave are you: free speech is not for you."

"Through not observing what is in the mind of another a man has seldom been seen to be unhappy; but those who do not observe the movements of their own minds must of necessity be unhappy."

"I can neither be injured by any of them, for no one can fix on me what is ugly, nor can I be angry with my kinsman, nor hate him. For we are made for co-operation, like feet, like hands, like eyelids, like the rows of the upper and lower teeth. To act against one another, then, is contrary to nature; and it is acting against one another to be vexed and to turn away."

"No man can rob us of our free will."

"From Sextus, a benevolent disposition, and the example of a family governed in a fatherly manner, and the idea of living comfortably to nature; and gravity without affectation, and to look carefully after the interests of friends, and to tolerate ignorant persons, and those who form opinions without consideration: he had the power of readily accommodating himself to all, so that intercourse with him was more agreeable than any flattery..."

"No longer talk at all about the kind of a man that a good man ought to be, but be such."

"What is your art? To be good. And how is this accomplished well except by general principles, some about the nature of the universe, and others about the proper constitution of man?"

"From Fronto[1] I learned to observe what envy, duplicity, and hypocrisy are in a tyrant, and that generally those among us who are called Patricians are rather deficient in paternal affection."

"From my brother Severus…consistency in disposition to do good, and to give to others readily and to cherish good hopes, and to believe that I am loved by my friends."

---

[1] *Fronto, named Marcus Cornelius Fronto, was Marcus Aurelius' tutor of law and Latin rhetoric.*

"If instead of a member, you say that you are merely a part, you have not as yet attained to a heartfelt love of mankind."

"What is my relation to men, and that we are made for one another; and in another respect, I was made to be set over them, as a ram over the flock or a bull over the herd. But examine the matter from first principles, from this. If all things are not mere atoms, it is nature which orders all things: if this is so, the inferior things exist for the sake of the superior, and these for the sake of one another."

"From Alexander the grammarian, to refrain from fault-finding, and not in a reproachful way to chide those who uttered any barbarous or selecistic or strange-sounding expression…"

"Men despise one another and flatter one another; and men wish to raise themselves above one another, and crouch before one another."

"Neither in writing nor in reading will you be able to lay down rules for others before you shalt have first learned to obey rules yourself. Much more is this so in life."

"Look down from above on the countless herds of men and their countless solemnities, and the infinitely varied voyagings in storms and calms, and the differences among those who are born, who live together, and die."

"If a man is mistaken, instruct him kindly and show him his error. But if you are not able, blame yourself, or blame not even yourself."

"What are these men's leading principles, and about what kind of things are they busy, and for what kind of reasons do they love and honor? Imagine that you see their poor souls laid bare. When they think that they do harm by their blame or good by their praise, what an idea!"

"It is your duty to leave another man's wrongful act there where it is."

"Do not look around you to discover other men's ruling principles, but look straight to this, to what nature leads you, both the universal nature through the things which happen to you, and your own nature through the acts which must be done by you. But every being ought to do that which is according to its constitution; and all other things have been constituted for the sake of rational beings, just as among irrational things the inferior for the sake of the superior, but the rational for the sake of one another."

"Remember this then, that this little compound, yourself, must either be dissolved, or your poor breath must be extinguished, or be removed and placed elsewhere."

"Every soul, the philosopher says, is involuntarily deprived of truth; consequently, in the same way it is deprived of justice and temperance and benevolence and everything of the kind. It is most necessary to bear this constantly in mind, for thus you wilt be more gentle towards all."

"The prime principle then in man's constitution is the social. And the second is not to yield to the persuasions of the body, for it is the peculiar office of the rational and intelligent motion to circumscribe itself, and never to be overpowered either by the intelligent motion claims superiority and does not permit for it is formed by nature to use all of them. The third thing in the rational constitution is freedom from error and from deception. Let then the ruling principle holding fast to these things go straight on, and it has what is its own."

"Penetrate inwards into men's leading principles, and you will see what judges you are afraid of, and what kind of judges they are of themselves."

"He often acts unjustly who does not do a certain thing; not only he who does a certain thing."

"He who does wrong does wrong against himself. He who acts unjustly acts unjustly to himself, because he makes himself bad."

Challenge: Strive to find the good in people. When interacting with others, focus only on what you can control. Use "I" statements to help you better take responsibility for your actions and refrain from blaming others.

III

CHASING FAME

FAME, RECOGNITION AND PLEASURE are
enjoyable yet fleeting moments in a life well-
lived. The goal of life is not to seek recognition
or rewards but to embody strong character traits
and live a virtuous life. Public opinion is no
more within your control than the opinions of
those around you; therefore, time and energy
should not be wasted on courting it. Pleasure
comes and goes and while it can provide you
with a boost of temporary happiness, true joy
and contentment comes from within. The
path to overall well-being is a personal, inward
journey, one that focuses on gratitude, self-con-
fidence, healthy relationships, self-direction, and
resilience.

Occupy your time and talents with meaningful and inspiring experiences, opportunities that
will better you and others in the long run. Avoid

the temptation towards instant gratification and instead direct your attention to those things that are within your control. Strive to do your best in every situation rather than hoping to win the praise of others. This effort-centric mindset will leave you feeling more fulfilled than any amount of outside acknowledgement.

Someday, we all reach our natural end. Anything that we obtain during our life will soon be forgotten. Your loved ones, your fans and followers will disappear in their time. How quickly all things disappear, so focus how you achieve personal success, rather than the success itself.

"Constantly bring to your recollection those who have complained greatly about anything, those who have been most conspicuous by the greatest fame or misfortunes or enmities or fortunes of any kind: then think where are they all now? Smoke and ash and a tale, or not even a tale."

"Contemplate the formative principles [forms] of things bare their coverings; the purposes of actions; consider what pain is, what pleasure is, and death, and fame; who is to himself the cause of his uneasiness; how no man is hindered by another; that everything is opinion."

"About fame: look at the minds [of those who seek fame], observe what they are, and what kind of things they avoid, and what kind of things they pursue. And consider that as the heaps of sand piled on one another hide the former sands, so in life the events which go before are soon covered by those which come after."

"Wipe out imagination; check desire; extinguish appetite; keep the ruling faculty in its own power."

"How many after being celebrated by fame have been given up to oblivion; and how many who have celebrated the fame of others have long been dead."

"Leaves, some the wind scatters on the ground—so is the race of men. Leaves, also, are your children; and leaves, too, are they who cry out so if they are worthy of credit, or bestow their praise, or on the contrary curse, or secretly blame and sneer; and leaves, in like manner, are those who shall receive and transmit a man's fame to after-times. For all such things as these 'are produced in the season of spring,' as the poet says; then the wind casts them down; then the forest produces other leaves in their places. But a brief existence is common to all things, and yet you avoid and pursue all things as if they would be eternal."

"That which is not good for the swarm, neither is it good for the bee."

"This reflection also tends to be the removal of the desire of empty fame, that is no longer on your power to have lived the whole of your life, or at least your life from the youth upwards, like a philosopher; but both too many others into yourself it is plain that you are from philosophy. You have fallen into disorder, then, so that is no longer easy for you to get the reputation of a philosopher; and the plan of your life also opposes it. If then you have truly seen where the matter lies, throw away the thought, how you shall seem, and be content if you shall live the rest of your life in such a wise as your nature wills."

"Let nothing else distract you; for you have had experience of many wanderings without having found happiness anywhere, not in syllogisms, nor in wealth, nor in reputation, nor an enjoyment, nor anywhere. Where is it then? In doing what man's nature requires. How then shall a man do this? If he has principles from which come his affects and his acts. What principles? Those which relate to good and bad the belief that there is nothing good for man which does not make him just, temperate, manly, free; and that there is nothing bad which does not do the contrary to what has been mentioned."

"Every nature is contented with itself when it goes on its way well; and a rational nature goes on way well when it confines its desires and aversions to the things which are in its power, and when it satisfied with everything that is assigned to it by the common nature. For this common nature every particular nature is a part, as the nature of the leaf is part of the nature of the plant; except that in the plant of the nature of the leaf is part of a nature which has not perception or reason, and is subject to be impeded; but the nature of man is part of a nature which is not subject to impediments, and is intelligent and just, since it gives everything an equal portions and according to its worth, times, substance, cause, activity, and incident. But examine, not to discover that anyone thing compared with any other single thing is equal and all respects, but by taking all the parts together of one thing and comparing them with all the parts together of another."

"Alexander and Caius and Pompeius, what are they in comparison with Diogenes and Heraclitus and Socrates? For they were acquainted with things, and their causes, in their matter, and the ruling principles of these men were the same. But as to the others, how many things had they care for, and to how many things were they slaves."

"Turn it inside out and see what kind of thing it is and when it has grown old, what kind of thing it becomes, and when it is diseased. short-lived or both appraiser and the praise, and the rememberer and the remembered: and all this in a nook of this part of the world; and not even here to do all agree, no, and not anyone with himself and the whole earth too is a point."

"Does Panthea or Fergamus now sit by the tomb of verses? Does Chaurias or Diotimus sit by the tomb of Hadrianus? That would be ridiculous. Well, suppose they did sit there, with the dead be conscious of it? if the dead were conscious, would they be pleased? if they were please, would that make them immortal? Was it not in the order of destiny that these persons too should first become old women and old men and then die? What then would those do after these were dead? all this is foul smell and blood in a bag."

"In the constitution of the rational animal I see no virtue which is opposed to justice; but I see a virtue which is opposed to love of pleasure, and that is temperance."

"Do not disturb yourself by thinking of the whole of your life. Let not your thoughts at once embrace all the various troubles which you mayest expect to befall you: but on every occasion ask yourself, what is there in this which is intolerable and past bearing? For that will be a shame to confess. in the next place remember that neither the future nor the past pains the but only the present. but this is reduced to a very little, if you only circumscribe it, and then chide your mind if it is unable to hold out against even this."

"Nature has regard and everything no less to the end than to the beginning and the continuance, just like the man who throws up a ball. what good is it then for the ball to be thrown up, or harm for it to come down, or even to have fallen? And what good is it to bubble while it holds together, or what harm when it is burst? The same may be said of a light also."

"Nature has not mingled with the composition of the body, as not to have allowed you power of circumscribing yourself and of bringing under subjections to yourself all that is your own; for it is very possible to be a Divine man and to be recognized as such by no one. Always be this in mind; and another thing too, that very little indeed is necessary for living a happy life. And because you have despaired of becoming a dialectician and skilled in the knowledge of nature, do not for this reason renounce the hope of being both free and modest, and social and obedient to god."

"For he who is excited by anger seems to turn away from reason with a certain pain and unconscious contraction; but he who offends through desire, being overpowered by pleasure, seems to be in a manner more intemperate and more womanish in his offenses."

"Have I done something for the general interest? Well then I have had my reward. Let this always be present to your mind, and never stop [doing such good]."

"Reflecting on all this, consider nothing to be great, except to act as your nature leads you, and to endure that which the common nature brings."

"Everything material soon disappears in the substance of the whole; and everything formal [causal] is very soon taken back into the universal reason; and the memory of everything is very soon overwhelmed in time."

"Such as bathing appears to you—oil, sweat, dirt, filthy water, all things disgusting—so is every part of life and everything."

"He who loves fame considers another man's activity to be his own good; and he who loves pleasure, his own sensations; but he who has understanding, considers his own acts to be his own good."

"As it happens to you in the amphitheater and such places, that the continual sight of the same things and the uniformity make the spectacle wearisome, so it is in the whole life; for all things above, below, are the same and from the same. How long then?"

"To seek what is impossible is madness: and it is impossible that the bad should not do smoothing of this kind."

"From the reputation and remembrance of my father, modesty and a manly character."

"From my mother, piety and beneficence, and abstinence, not only from evil deeds, but even from evil thoughts; and further, simplicity in my way of living, far removed from the habits of the rich."

"Think continually that all kinds of men and of all kinds of pursuits and of all nations are dead."

"How easy it is to repel and to wipe away every impression which is troublesome or unsuitable, and immediately to be in all tranquility."

"What we do now echoes in eternity."

"Let no act be done without a purpose, nor otherwise than according to the perfect principles of art."

"From Diognetus,[2] not to busy myself about trifling things, and not to give credit to what was said by miracle-workers and jugglers."

[2] *One of Marcus Aurelius' tutors.*

"Nothing is needed by fools, for they do not understand how to use anything, but are in want of everything."

"Don't be whirled about, but in every movement have respect for justice, and on the occasion of every impression maintain the faculty of comprehension."

"Be indifferent to what makes no difference."

"Pleasures, when they go beyond a certain limit, are but punishments."

"It is your duty to order your life well in every single act."

Challenge: Make it a habit to do something for yourself each week. Make that something be something that makes you feel fulfilled without any recognition. View acts as a means to live a purposeful and meaningful life, not an end to a means filled with public rewards.

IV

LIVING WITH NATURE

MARCUS AURELIUS' USE OF the term "nature" included not only the natural world, but also human nature and the nature of the universe. The goal of the Stoic lifestyle is to purposely and deliberately live your life in agreement with nature. This allows you to accept the world around you, increase your resilience, and live a happier life as a result.

The Stoics believed individual human nature is part of a greater universal nature. To live in agreement with nature makes it easier to accept what is not within your control and to acknowledge that everything around you is subject to change through forces you have no say over. Coping with change can be difficult for many, but fully embracing the concept of living in agreement with nature will help you accept the surprises that occur in your life and give you the ability to view things through a different lens.

To live in agreement with nature is to a deeper understanding of yourself and society as a whole. Nature is not chaos; it serves as a guiding force, an anchor in an ever-changing and dynamic world. Strive to understand your place in the world and allow nature to be your virtuous guide on the way to living a more harmonious and thoughtful life.

"The first step: Don't be anxious. Nature controls it all."

"This you must always bear in mind: what is the nature of the whole, and what is my nature, and how this is related to that, and what kind of a part it is of what kind of a whole; and that there is no one who hinders you from always doing and saying the things which are according to the nature of which you are a part."

"But that is good for every part of nature which the nature of the whole brings, and what serves to maintain this nature."

"In conformity to the nature of the universe every single thing is accomplished, for certainly it is not in conformity to any other nature that each thing is accomplished, either a nature which externally comprehends this, or a nature which is comprehended with this nature, or a nature external and independent of this."

"The universe is either a confusion, and a mutual involution of things, and a dispersion; or it is unity and order and providence."

"And why am I disturbed, for the disposition of my elements will happen whatever I do?"

"He who acts unjustly acts impiously. For since universal nature has made rational animals for the sake of one another, to help one another according to their deserts, but in no way to injure one another, he who transgresses her will is clearly guilty of impiety towards the highest divinity."

"To look for a fig in winter is a madman's act; such is he who looks for his child when it is no longer allowed."

"And further, this universal nature is named truth, and is the prime cause of all things that are true."

"No man is tired of receiving what is useful. But it is useful to act according to nature. Do not then be tired of receiving what is useful by doing it to others."

"It is Nature's work to transfer what is now here into another place, to change things, to carry them hence, and set them elsewhere."

"The nature of the universal has this work to do, to remove to that place the things which are in this, to change them, to take them away hence, and to carry them there."

"All that exists is the seed of what will emerge from it."

"The nature of the All moved to make the universe. But now either everything that takes place comes by way of consequence or [continuity]; or even the chief things towards which the ruling power of the universe directs its own movement are governed by no rational principle. If this is remembered, it will make you more tranquil in many things."

"Confine yourself to the present."

"Whatever the rational and political [social] faculty finds to be neither intelligent nor social, it properly judges to be inferior to itself."

"Men seek out retreats for themselves in the country, by the seaside, on the mountains... Nowhere can a man find a retreat more peaceful or more free from trouble than his own soul."

"He is at war with Nature who sets himself against the truth."

"Misfortune nobly born is good fortune."

"This thing, what is it in itself, in its own constitution?"

Challenge: Set a goal to spend at least fifteen minutes each day outside and enjoying nature. Take this time to practice self-reflection and appreciate your place in the universe.

V

RULES FOR LIVING WELL

A LIFE WELL LIVED IS a life rich in the Stoic virtues of wisdom, justice, courage, and temperance. Wisdom is knowing the difference between good and bad and making logical and rational decisions. Wisdom strengthens your ability to be in control of your emotions and make thoughtful choices. Living a just life applies your ability to judge between good and bad actions and choose to do what is right, especially during difficult times. Courage is what gives you the strength needed to act justly in trying and uncertain times. Temperance, also referred to as moderation, can be understood as living a life free from indulgence—a virtuous life of contentment and happiness, not one filled with short-term pleasures.

If you live a virtuous life and remind yourself of these four pillars of Stoicism, you will be better prepared to use reason and rationality while thoughtfully choosing your reactions and responses. Your thoughts have the power to influence every aspect of your life, with positive and rational thoughts naturally creating a positive life. A rational mind allows you to view situations and circumstances in a calm and careful manner.

Marcus Aurelius knew the importance of rational thinking and not allowing your emotions to control you. Better decisions are made when emotions are well regulated. Your rational mind is responsible for your judgment, reactions, and responses. Attempt to make future decisions based on clear thinking, rationality, and realism, not emotions or impulses. Becoming the master of your mind will make you feel more in control of situations that may come your way.

"The first rule is to keep an untroubled spirit. The second is to look things in the face and know them for what they are."

"Adorn yourself with simplicity and modesty and with indifference towards the things which lie between virtue and vice. Love mankind. Follow God. The poet says that law rules all—And it is enough to remember that law rules all."

"Don't allow yourself to be heard any longer griping about public life, not even with your own ears!"

"Always run to the short way; and the short way is the natural: accordingly say and do everything in conformity with the soundest reason. For such a purpose frees a man from trouble, and warfare, and all artifice and ostentatious display."

"In the morning when you awake unwillingly, let this thought be present: 'I am rising to the work of a human being.'"

"Consider that everything is opinion, and opinion is in your power."

"Take away your opinion, and then there is taken away the complaint, 'I have been harmed. Take away the complaint, 'I have been harmed,' and the harm is taken away."

"That which does not make a man worse than he was, also does not make his life worse, nor does it harm him either from without or from within."

"Do you not see the little plants, the little birds, the ants, the spiders, the bees working together to put in order their several parts of the universe?"

"The substance of the universe is obedient and compliant; and the reason which governs it has in itself no cause for doing evil, for it has no malice, nor does it do evil to anything, nor is anything harmed by it. But all things are made and perfected according to this reason."

"We must endure, and toil without complaining."

"You can pass your life in an equable flow of happiness, if you can go by the right way, and think and act in the right way."

"Life must be reaped like the ripe ears of corn:
One man is born; another dies."

"If it's endurable, then endure it, stop
complaining."

"It is man's special business to love even those
who err; and to this love you attain, if it is
borne in upon you that even these sinners
are your kin, and that they offend through
ignorance and against their will."

"Adapt yourself to the things which your destiny has given you: love those with whom it is your lot to live, and love them with sincere affection."

"No joining others in their wailing, no violent emotion."

"If it is not right, do not do it, if it is not true, do not say it."

"Try to persuade men to agree with you; but whether they agree or not, pursue the course you have marked out when the principles of justice point that way."

"From Antisthenes: It is royal to do good and to be abused."

"Do you exist then to take your pleasure, and not all for action or exertion?"

"Today I have escaped from all trouble; or rather I have cast out all trouble from me. For it was not without but within, in my own opinions."

"The best way of avenging yourself is not to become like [the wrong doer]."

"Look within. Let neither the peculiar quality of anything nor its value escape you."

"You have forgotten, too, that it is the present moment only that one can live or lose."

"To have good fortune is to have a good spirit, or a good mind."

"Let no man have it in his power to say with truth of you that you are not a man of simplicity, candor, and goodness."

"The ruling principle is that which rouses and turns itself, and while it makes itself such as it and such as it wills to be, it also makes everything which happens appear to itself to be such as it wills."

"Does anyone hate me? That is his affair. I shall be kind and good-natured to everyone."

"See things again as once you saw them, and your life is made new again."

"It is neither the past nor the future that can oppress you, but always be the present only."

"The perfection of moral character consists in this, in passing every day as the last, and in being neither violently excited nor torpid nor playing the hypocrite."

"It is not right to vex ourselves at things, for they care nought about it."

"Be satisfied if the smallest thing go well."

"Take pleasure in one thing and rest in it, in passing from one social act to another social act, thinking of god."

"Look within. Within is the fountain of good, and it will ever bubble up, if you would ever dig."

"Receive [wealth or prosperity] without arrogance; and be ready to let it go."

"Men exist for the sake of one another. Teach them then, or bear with them."

"Enter into every man's ruling faculty; and also let every other man enter into thine."

"If any man is able to convince me and show me that I do not think or act right, I will gladly change; for I seek the truth, by which no man was ever injured. But he is injured who abides in his error and ignorance. But he is injured who abides in his error and ignorance."

Challenge: Remind yourself of the four Stoic Virtues, wisdom, justice, courage, and temperance, and make it a goal to live virtuously by incorporating each into your daily routine.

VI

LIFE IS SHORT

MARCUS AURELIUS WAS KEENLY aware of the fact that life is short and unpredictable. Change *will* occur, whether you want it to or not. The one and only thing you have total and complete control over is yourself: your thoughts, your behaviors, your responses, your actions, and your judgments. Knowing this, strive to possess an appreciative view of life while acknowledging that nothing lasts forever.

It's important to focus on the present and realize it is but a fleeting moment that will never exist again. This perspective may at first bring about a rush of negative emotions, but this is only do to a lingering desire for unrealistic control. Instead, let these truths motivate you to make the most out of life. Accepting that life is short gives you the freedom to fully experience occurrences, practice mindfulness, and be in the moment. The act of being in the present lets you completely immerse yourself in that situation. You will have a greater appreciation and understanding of most things if you are able to give it your full attention. Free yourself from distractions and nonessential irrelevant thoughts.

Respect the time you have on this Earth by valuing each day and each moment. See the beauty and good in all things and refrain from wanting more. Time is precious and must not be wasted. Don't wish your life away.

"But thine is nearly finished, though your soul reverences not itself, but places your felicity in the souls of others."

"Remember how long you have been putting off these things, and how often you have received an opportunity from the gods, and yet do not use it."

"Begin the morning by saying to yourself, I shall meet with the busybody, the ungrateful, arrogant, deceitful, envious, unsocial."

"Consider in what condition both in body and soul man should be when he's overtaken by death; and consider the shortness of life, the boundless abyss of time past and future, the feebleness of all matter."

"Through the universal substance as through a furious torrent all bodies are carried, being by their nature united with and co-operating with the whole, as the parts of our body with one another. How many a Chrysippus, how many a Socrates, how many an Epictetus has time already swallowed up! And let the same thought occur to you with reference to every man and thing."

"Do not look around the to discover other men's ruling principles, but look straight to this, to what nature leads the, both the universal nature through the things which happen to be the, and your own nature through the ax which must be done by you. but every being ought to do that which is according to its constitution; and all of the things have been constituted for the sake of rational beings, just as among irrational things the inferior for the sake of the superior, but the rational for the sake of one another."

"Another may be more expert in casting his opponent; but he is not more social, nor more modest, or better discipline to meet all that happens, more considerate with respect to the faults of his neighbors."

"All existing things soon changed, and they will either be reduced to vapour, if indeed all substance is one, or they will be dispersed."

"It is a shame for the soul to be first to give way in this life, when your body does not give way."

"Your days are numbered. Use them to throw open the windows of your soul to the sun. If you do not, the sun will soon set, and you with it."

"Think of yourself as dead. You have lived your life. Now take what's left and live it properly."

"When you are vexed or worried overmuch, remember that man's life is but for a moment, and that in a little we shall all be laid to rest."

"Before all things be not perturbed. Everything comes to pass as directed by universal Nature, and in a little time you will be departed and gone, like Hadrianus and Augustus."

"You have to assemble your life yourself, action by action."

"Dwell not on what you lack so much as on what you have already."

"Retire into yourself."

"Wipe out the imagination. Stop the pulling of the strings. Confine yourself to the present."

"Ask yourself at every moment, is this necessary?"

"If gods care not for me and my children. There is no reason for it."

"Direct your attention to what is said."

"For the good is with me, and the just."

"Just that you do the right thing. The rest doesn't matter."

"Every hour, focus your mind attentively... on the performance of the task in hand, with dignity, human sympathy, benevolence and freedom, and leave aside all other thoughts. You will achieve this, if you perform each action as if it were your last."

Challenge: Create a gratitude journal and identify those things for which you are grateful. Write in your journal a few times a week and review it often.

VII

ON DEATH

DEATH AWAITS EACH OF us at the end of our life's journey. There's no escaping it; our time in this life is as precious as it is finite. With this understanding, seek to live in harmony with your circumstances. While death is not something most people enjoy discussing, Marcus' conversations and writings to himself reflect his belief that we should fear living an unfulfilled life, rather than fear death itself. Accepting our mortality will help guide us to a greater understanding of why death is not to be feared. We must accept and acknowledge what is to come and strive to be present in order to live a more mindful and purposeful life.

"Every soul, the philosopher says, is involuntarily deprived of truth; consequently in the same way it is deprived of justice and temperance and benevolence and everything of the kind. It is most necessary to bear this constantly in mind, for the style wilt be more gentle towards all."

"How do we know if Telauges was not superior in character to Socrates? For it is not enough that Socrates died a more noble death, and disputed more skillfully with sophists, and passed the night in the cold with more endurance, and that when he was bid to arrest Leon of Salamis, he considered it more noble to refuse, and that he walked in a swaggering way in the streets though as to this fact one may have great doubts if it was true."

"But we ought to inquire, what kind of soul it was that Socrates possessed, and if he was able to be content with being just towards men and pious towards the gods, neither I believe vexed on account of men's villainy, nor yet making himself a slave to any man's ignorance, nor receiving as strange anything that felt is sure out of the universal, nor enduring it as intolerable, we're allowing his understanding to sympathize with the affects of the miserable flesh."

"Death is a cessation of the impressions through the senses, and of the pulling of the strings which move the appetites, and of the discursive movements of the thoughts, and of the service to the flesh."

"Do not act as if you were going to live ten thousand years. Death hangs over you. While you live, while it is in your power, be good."

"You have existed as a part. You shall disappear in that which produced you; but rather you shall be received back into its seminal principle by transmutation."

"It is natural that these things should be done by such persons, it is a matter of necessity; and if a man will not have it so, he will not allow the fig-tree to have juice. But by all means bear this in mind, that within a very short time both you and he will be dead; and soon not even your names will be left behind."

"Many grains of frankincense on the same altar: one falls before another falls after; but it makes no difference."

"He who fears death either fears the loss of sensation or a different kind of sensation."

"He who has a vehement desire for posthumous fame does not consider that every one of those who remember him will himself also die very soon; then again also they who have succeeded them, un the whole remembrance shall have been extinguished as it is transmitted through men who foolishly admire and perish. But suppose that those who will remember are even immortal, and that the remembrance will be immortal, what then is this to you? And I say not what is it to the dead, but what is it to the living. What is praise, except indeed so far as it has a certain utility? For you now reject unseasonably the gift of nature, clinging to something else..."

"Soon, very soon, you will be ashes, or a skeleton, and either a name or not even a name; but name is sound and echo. And the things which are much valued in life are empty and rotten and trifling, and like little dogs biting one another, and little children quarreling, laughing, and then straightway weeping. But fidelity and modesty and justice and truth are fled."

"All that you see will quickly perish, and those who have been spectators of its dissolution will very soon perish, too. And he who dies at the extremest old age will be brought into the same condition with him who died prematurely."

"Throw away your books; no longer distract yourself: it is not allowed; but as if you were now dying, despise the flesh; it is blood and bones and network, a contexture of nerves, veins, and arteries."

"Alexander the Macedonian and his groom by death were brought to the same state; for either they were received among the same seminal principles of the universe, or they were alike dispersed among the atoms."

"Mimi, War, astonishment, torpor, slavery, will daily wipe out those holy principles of thine."

"Look at everything that exists, and observe that it is already in dissolution and in change, and as it were putrefaction or dispersion, or that everything is so constituted by nature as to die."

"About death: whether it is a dispersion, or a resolution into atoms, or annihilation, it is either extinction or change."

"Imagine every man who is grieved at anything or discontented to be a pig which is sacrificed and kicks and screams."

"The time is at hand when you shall forget all things, and when all shall forget you."

"Consider each of the things around you as already dissolving, in a state of change, and as it were corrupting and being dissipated, or as, one and all, formed by nature to die."

"This from Plato: 'To the man who has true grandeur of mind, and who contemplates all time and all being, can human life appear a great matter?' Impossible says the other. 'Can then such a one count death a thing of dread?' Not indeed.'"

"From Plato: 'I would make him this just answer, 'you are mistaken, my friend, to think that a man of any worth should count the chances of living and dying. Should he not rather, in all he does, consider simply whether he is acting justly of unjustly, whether he is playing the part of a good man or a bad.'"

"Loss is naught but change; in change is the joy of universal Nature, and by her all things are ordered well."

"Pause and ask yourself if death is a dreadful thing because it deprives you of this."

"That which has grown from the earth to the
earth,
But that which has sprung from
heavenly seed,
Back to the heavenly realms returns.
This is either dissolution of the mutual
involution of the atoms, or a similar
dispersion of the unsentient elements."

"Despise not death; but receive it well content, as one of the things which Nature wills."

"Death smiles at us all, but all a man can do is smile back."

"The memory of all things is quickly buried in eternity."

"Death is such as a generation is, a mystery of nature; composition out of the same elements, and a decomposition into the same; and altogether not a thing of which any man should be ashamed, for it is not contrary to [the nature of] a reasonable animal, and not contrary to the reason of our constitution."

Challenge: Take time each day to appreciate the present moment. Realize this moment is uniquely wonderful and will never occur again. Acknowledge that your time here on this earth is precious and motivate yourself to make the most of it every single day.

Final Thoughts

CHOOSE TO INCORPORATE MARCUS Aurelius' wise, Stoic-inspired words into your own journey to shift and shape your rules for daily living. Our hope is that the wisdom, courage, justice, and temperance found within these pages may serve as a cornerstone for a more deliberate way of life. This book is meant to be a tool that is easily referenced and frequently revisited. Use this book to reframe your lens and integrate his beliefs, lessons and experiences into your own life.

Living virtuously as Marcus Aurelius did will allow you to accept change and better deal with people and situations that are not within your control. This Stoic mindset enables the kind of focus necessary to appreciate what is truly important in life and teaches you how to be content with what you have.

In fact, appreciation is a key component in living in agreement with nature and accepting the world around you while still valuing and cherishing each moment. There are few who understood this as well as Marcus Aurelius, and we are grateful for having had the chance to share his thoughts with you. Thank you for taking the time to read our interpretation of Marcus Aurelius' personal writings; may they serve to guide your way towards a more purposeful existence.

About the Authors

Nick Benas grew up in Guilford, Connecticut. A former United States Marine Sergeant and Iraq Combat Veteran, Nick is a 2nd Dan Black Belt in Tae Kwon-Do and a Green Belt Instructor in the Marine Corps Martial Arts Program. He holds an undergraduate degree in Sociology and an MS in Public Policy from Southern Connecticut State University. He has been featured for his business success and entrepreneurship by more than 50 major media outlets, including Entrepreneur Magazine, Men's Health, ABC, FOX, ESPN, and CNBC. His passion lies in serving veterans and writing.

Kortney Yasenka, LCMHC, is a licensed clinical mental health counselor who provides individual, family, and group therapy, as well as life coaching services. Kortney is certified in trauma-focused cognitive behavioral therapy and incorporates physical activity and eco-therapy into counseling and coaching sessions. She has a Masters in Counseling Psychology with a concentration in Health Psychology from

Northeastern University. With over 15 years of experience, Kortney has worked in community mental health, school systems, and private practice. In her free time, she enjoys running, spending time with family, and vacationing on the beautiful island of St. John.

Also by Nick Benas

The Stoicism Book of Quotes
The Warrior's Book of Virtues
Mental Health Emergencies
Tactical Mobility
Warrior Wisdom
The Resilient Warrior

Also by Kortney Yasenka

The Stoicism Book of Quotes
Swedish Lagom